Guide to
The Rossendale Way

Guide to
The Rossendale Way

Jack Woods

Published by Sigma Leisure – an imprint of
Sigma Press, Stobart House, Pontyclerc, Penybanc Road
Ammanford, Carmarthenshire SA18 3HP

British Library Cataloguing in Publication Data

A CIP record for this book is available from the British Library

ISBN: 978-1-85058-894-8

Typesetting and Design by: Sigma Press, Ammanford, Carms

Maps: © Jack Woods

Photographs: © Jack Woods

Cover photograph: The junction of the RW with Rooley Moor Road near Top of Leach

Printed by: Berforts Group Ltd, Stevenage

Disclaimer: The information in this book is given in good faith and is believed to be correct at the time of publication. Care should always be taken when walking in hill country. Where appropriate, attention has been drawn to matters of safety. The author and publisher cannot take responsibility for any accidents or injury incurred whilst following these walks. Only you can judge your own fitness, competence and experience. Do not rely solely on sketch maps for navigation: we strongly recommend the use of appropriate Ordnance Survey (or equivalent) maps.

Contents

Introduction

When walking along the Rossendale Way a few years ago I used the Ordnance Survey West Pennine Moors and the South Pennines maps, and a series of pamphlets I bought at Clough Head Information Centre at Haslingden Grane. I was struck by the beauty of most of the forty-five mile route, with extensive views on fine days, and the wealth of fascinating archaeological, social and industrial history to be explored. The leaflets described the route in eight stages, and were based on the excellent books by Ian Goldthorpe, Rossendale Rambles and Further Rossendale Rambles, (see under General Information at the back of the book). These guides to practically every footpath in the Borough of Rossendale were a tour de force and the Rossendale equivalent of Wainwright's Lake District guides. They have been out of print for some time but copies occasionally turn up in second-hand book shops. It is difficult to imagine how they could be bettered in the historical details, and the superb sketches and photographs; but there have been a number of changes to footpaths, buildings, public transport etc since the initial publication. This applies also to the leaflets, of course. More changes will occur if quarrying along the northern side of Haslingden Grane is drastically extended.

In addition, the Rossendale Way is described only in an anti-clockwise direction as a result of the footpath signs (where there are any) having been erected that way along the route. The RW is most likely to be walked in sections, apart from the annual 'Rossendale Way in a Day' challenge in aid of Rossendale Mountain Rescue; there are few places along the Way where overnight accommodation can be obtained. Some starting places are not easily accessible by public transport on all days of the week, so walkers will need to reverse their route in order to get back to a starting point. It may, on occasions, be more convenient to walk clockwise and return the other way. Bus services vary from season to season so I have provided web-site addresses and telephone numbers at the back of the book.

I wanted to produce a new guide which would describe the Rossendale Way in both directions, but it meant, of course, much duplication of descriptions of what can be seen along the route. Reluctantly, therefore, I decided to follow the original anti-clockwise guide because the vast majority of Rossendale Way direction signs point that way. Mind you, another reason for producing a new guide is that there are many path junctions where no guide post exists at all, (Ending Rake in Healey is a typical example; along the footpath between Middle Hill and Hades Hill is another.) In spite of a number of representations I made to Groundwork Rossendale and Lancashire County Council, virtually no improvement has been made to this state of affairs. I was told that funds would be available for it in 2007 but it never happened. An OS map is therefore desirable, even when using this guide.

I have divided the Rossendale Way into nine sections, each starting and finishing at a motor road for consistency. This makes one or two sections very short but this can be ideal for those people just spending a few hours walking the route especially when a return to the car must be made.

Since the body of this guide was written certain sections of the Rossendale Way have been newly signed, particularly between Love Clough and Clough Head.

I have tried to avoid infringing any copyright, and also to make sure that the 'official' route is described accurately, and that my directions refer to true public rights of way. If there are mistakes please inform me through the publisher.

I would like to thank Colin Rathbone for the painstaking drawing of the maps, and Arnold Sampson, footpath secretary for the Rossendale branch of the Ramblers Association, for being brave enough to undertake the proof-reading of my text. I should also like to thank Ian Davies, former footpaths officer for the LCC, who helped in attempting to resolve a dog problem along the route.

My real debt is to Mr C K Lee, to whom I owe my deep love of the Lake Distict which began with one of the KGS master's walking tours in 1955.

Jack Woods
August 2011

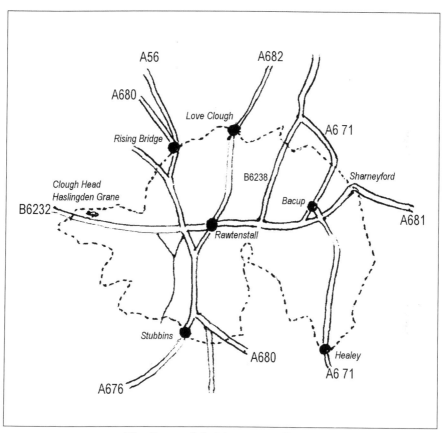

The Rossendale Way – overall map

1. Clough Head, Haslingden Grane, to Stubbins

approximately 9 miles (14.5km)

Clough Head car park and Information Centre, just off the busy B6232 (not A6177 as on the latest OS map) Haslingden to Blackburn Road, is an excellent place to start a number of walks as well as the Rossendale Way. There are clean toilets, a good café, and leaflets and information about events in the area. Make sure you know at what time the barrier to the car park closes: if you're late back you may find your car locked in. If needing to return to a vehicle at the end of the day and eighteen miles (29km) is too much, then I suggest Great House Farm, which is just about 5 miles (8km), as the turning point. The remaining part of the section can be walked later by accessing the RW at Great House from the White Horse, on the B6235 Holcombe Road, in Helmshore.

Clough Head Café and Information Centre

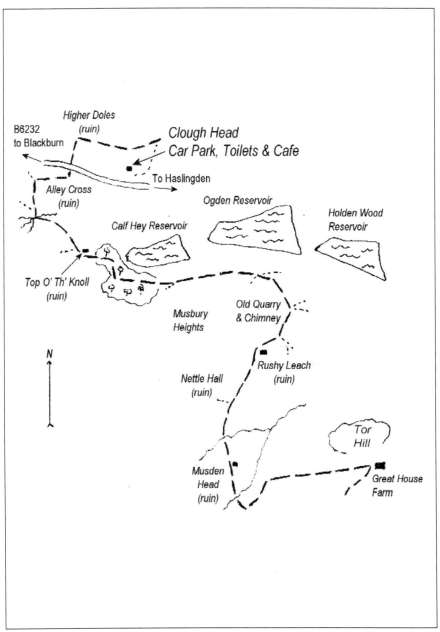

Clough Head, Haslingden Grane, to Great House Farm

Jamestone Quarry, Clough Head

To reach the RW take the track to the right of the building to a metal kissing gate. Then follow the track to where it bends left round a wood. Here is the site of Grane Brickworks, opened in 1895, which did not last more than a few years. Turn left on the farm track and then right at a field gate, take a concessionary path by the fence to a metal kissing gate or stile and follow the path through the small conifer wood. The path emerges at the top end of the wood at an information board about the history of quarrying. The water-filled Jamestone Quarry is down on the right, the stratification of the rock which underlies the moorland very evident. Stone from this area, known locally as 'lonky', would split easily due to the natural effect of water and frost and came to be used for pavements in many parts of the UK and abroad. Pass over a stile and head up the field till you reach a crossing path by a broken wall. You are now on the RW.

1. Turn left on an overgrown track . The 1846 Ordnance Survey map
    shows this hillside as 'Fowl Edge', while by 1895 it is shown as
    'Foe Edge'. We shall come across another 'Foe' or 'Fo' Edge near
    Scout Moor on the next leg of the circuit. The ruin you pass on
    the left is of the former Middle Foe Edge Farm.

2. Next comes a wooden kissing gate, and a stone step stile at a
    substantial wall corner. The old lane surface beyond is mostly firm
    but for views over the six feet (2m) high wall you should make your
    way up on the right bank. You can see the whole of the head of
    Grane, with Hog Lowe Pike and its OS column quite prominent, and
    further west the TV masts on Winter Hill. Much of the length of
    this track right up to Souter Hill at the head of Grane was laid out
    as a road when the edges of Haslingden Common were enclosed
    in the early 17th century, intended only for the use of those people
    living on adjoining land. The road was officially closed later
    because the locals of Grane found its maintenance, in addition to
    the usual road lower down the valley, too expensive. By the time
    the first 1:10 000 OS map was produced the road was marked as
    merely a footpath. After passing above a wood take the stile over
    the wall onto the scanty remains of Higher Doles Farm, noting the
    stone water trough, and walk straight down to the road. On the
    left among trees are the sites of The Hare and Hounds Inn and a
    smithy, both shown on early OS maps.

3. Cross the busy road, turn left, and in a few yards take a signed
    lane on the right, then right again along a well defined track.
    Continue to the site of Alley Cross farm, where a stone cross used
    to stand; 'Alley' is a corruption of the word 'Holy'. Two German
    prisoners of war who had escaped from a camp near Bury were
    recaptured here in November 1944. An old lane used to go off to
    the right up over Souter Hill, but this is now a mere footpath to
    the present main road. Where the old rush filled farm track drops
    between banks, the RW bears left, cutting the corner, as indicated
    by an RW post.

4. Rejoining the track bear left along it to pass through the ruins of
    Bottom of the Rough. Beyond, the original lane surface has
    disappeared under marshy turf and rushes, and where it starts to
    descend between high banks keep up on the east (left) side until

you reach an RW sign. The old lane continued straight on here to the next farm. It is now a stream passing through pipes. Turn right to a second waymarker which points left along the hillside.

5. There is not much of a path and the ground can be heavily waterlogged, even after a reasonably dry period. Locate another post on drier ground, and then head for trees and the ruin of Close Bottom Farm.

6. Passing on, once again the lane between broken walls has become a stream bed, but it's possible to walk above it to reach the next ruin, that of Peak Farm, where there is a board with interesting information about the whisky distillers of Grane.

7. The old lane, now firm underfoot, soon drops towards Top O' Th' Knoll, which still retains walls up to 20 feet (6m) high. A fence directs the path away to the right for safety, taking you round to

Top O' th' Knoll, where 'Owd Andrey' built a cart in his living room

the front of the ruin, and then down steps and over a stream. The old lane would have passed through the farm yard and you can see its continuation up the slope beyond, now completely overgrown with rushes. The greatest character of old Grane lived at this farm in the nineteenth century. 'Owd Andrey', as he was known, was a true eccentric and loner. He is said to have built a cart in his front room, only to find it was too wide to pass through the doorway! Rather than dismantle either the cart or the doorway he kept it there, without wheels, and it became so well known that people came from miles around specially to see it, although Andrew closed up the window with stones.

8. After crossing the stream climb up to rejoin the old track, and then pass through a kissing gate into a conifer wood. The RW turns right (RW sign) along the old track through the trees. After two large stone gateposts descend left with an old delph on your right, where there is a wooden seat from which there is a fine view over Ogden Reservoir towards Cribden, overlooking Haslingden. Descend a twisting track past some interesting mushroom-like sculptures. Note the overgrown cartway is now down on the right.

Footbridge near Calf Hey Reservoir

9. At the bottom of the slope the old track turns left and passes between the ruins of Grane Head. At an RW post, you turn right along a clear wide path to some steps. The RW sign here points the wrong way, so ignore it and descend the steps to a footbridge. After crossing the stream a left turn would take you to a footpath alongside Calf Hey Reservoir, where, if it is a Sunday, you might meet a number of people strolling with their dogs.

10. The RW, however, turns right and continues along a pleasant path with a conifer wood on the left and a small stream on the right. More steps lead down to another bridge over another stream which runs down to Calf Hey Reservoir. There is a lunch table and benches. The RW turns sharp right after the footbridge. At an RW sign a clear track can be seen ascending by the stream, with the scant remains of Clough Side on the left, but the RW turns left below the ruin. To the left is an open view of the valley and Ogden Reservoir.

11. Soon pass through a kissing gate to another footbridge and you are then on Access Land. Views open out over the whole Grane valley, and you can see the line of the Rossendale Way from above Clough Head, along Foe Edge, eastwards past Deep Clough, and on to Windy Harbour.

12. Another ruin is passed, this one of Northampton Farm, and then a Peak and Northern Footpath sign. This indicates a sharp right turn up the steep hillside over to Edgworth, and the path we have come along to Hoddlesden. A few yards further another P & N sign by a tall tree indicates a path to Calf Hey Reservoir. Neither indicates the RW. Another kissing gate comes next, with an RW post built into it. Carry on along the terraced path past Under Heights ruin and in a few yards the RW drops down to ford a stream and arrives at a junction of paths.

13. The RW post here is slightly misleading, as it appears to point down to the reservoir level. In fact, the RW ascends the eroded path up the hillside.

14. So, girding up your loins, take the right hand path, and where it swings right pause to admire the panorama over the valleys. To the west the line of the RW can be seen from the head of Grane,

Holden Wood reservoir and Haslingden from the path up to Musbury Heights

past Foe Edge, Deep Clough, and Windy Harbour, climbing over the lower slopes of Thirteen Stone Hill towards Rising Bridge. Over Holden Wood Reservoir, beyond Haslingden, Cribden is prominent, and further east and south the line of the RW appears again, above Bacup, over Hades Hill with the Pennines beyond. Further, you can see it around Cowpe Lowe, along Foe Edge by Waugh's Well, and disappearing round the back of Scout Moor above Edenfield and Stubbins. Wonderful on a bright and clear day; a vista almost completely hidden under industrial haze from the middle of the nineteenth century until a few decades ago.

15. Follow the path up the hill and over a ruined wall to an old stone gate post, then follow the path round to the right. Suddenly you are on Musbury Heights, and there before you is the partly restored chimney of the quarry scrubbing mill, which you may have seen from the RW on the north side of Grane. The broken

walls of the old quarry workings here have been 'tidied up', probably for safety as far as the chimney is concerned, which was left in a dangerous state after being struck by lightning in 1983.

16. The way through the quarry workings is a bit confusing and, as I write, there are no RW signs to help. With your back to the path you have just ascended go left, ignoring any paths off to the right until you have passed through a short cutting in the embankment of a dismantled tramway. After a few yards the RW turns right by a small ruin and continues between high spoil heaps. Soon it bears left and passes by a deep quarry hole, where gigantic blocks of stone are piled. The track ends just before a wall corner, where there is a stile with an RW post. Once over the stile pause to admire the view into the lovely Musbury Valley. Two of the three mills, initially water powered, which were in operation in the valley in the first part of the nineteenth century, were already in ruins by 1900. The lower part of Musbury Brook had several

The reconstructed scrubbing mill chimney on Musbury Heights

artificial but delightful waterfalls, and I can remember as a young boy of five sitting by the stream listening to the gurgle of the water and watching brown trout lazing between the stones. Unfortunately, a severe storm in July 1964 produced such a rush of water that the falls were torn out and a working mill near Holcombe Road was flooded. The valley has never looked quite the same since, although it is still a lovely place.

17. The RW drops gently ahead down to the ruins of Rushy Leach, the ditch and bank joining from your right being the remains of part of the boundary of a large medieval deer park. Extending across the slopes of Grane to the heights of Tor Hill, the deer park was enclosed by the Earl of Lincoln, Lord of the Manor of Tottington, in 1304. A bank and ditch were constructed around the 4½ mile (7km) perimeter, which was topped by a tall strong fence. 'Deer leaps' were constructed which allowed deer to get in, but not out, and so new blood was constantly added to the herd. By 1507, however, Musbury Park was said to be waste ground 'now laid to pasture'.

Musbury Tor from Rushy Leach

Musbury Valley from Musden Head. What a view from the farm!

18. Soon passing under the ruins of Musden Head on the right, continue along the embankment to the site of Nettle Hall, where the boundary of the old deer park can be seen heading down across the valley.

19. Pass through what was the farmyard, and then keep a wall on your right as you continue. (The OS map shows the RW to the right of the wall but the track is overgrown and choked with rushes.) On the steep hillside above can be seen another ruin known locally as 'Causey End'.

    The RW drops down to cross what I take to be the main tributary of Musbury Brook. At a gateway an old disused track comes down from the right: Bailiff's Rake was the old cartway leading from round the head of the valley up the hillside to Causeway End. Continuing, you come to a substantial ruin, another Musden Head. (There were two farms of that name marked on the 1846 map, but

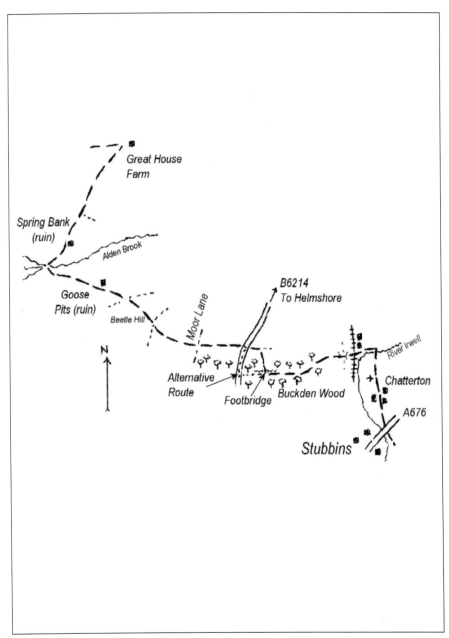

Great House Farm to Stubbins

only the one above Rushy Leach is so marked on today's.) There is another stream to cross where the track drops down to the wall corner. I think there must have been a culvert here that has been blocked, so Long Grain Water now runs across the track. Round the corner the wall has fallen, and it is below here that evidence for the culvert can be seen.

20. Continue up the track and pass the ruins of Burnt Hill on the left near the line of the south-eastern section of the fourteenth century deer park boundary that you walked along between Rushy Leach and Nettle Hall. There is scant visible evidence of it today. The RW is easy to follow to the top of the rise, where it crosses a small stream and a broken wall before turning left between a fence and a wall.

21. At an access notice a kissing gate leads to a stile and the RW then crosses a field slightly right to a second stile. After this it continues direction to a gateway, and on past a small wood. Note on the left the moorland reclaimed as pasture which leads up to the craggy top of Musbury Tor. There is no public access from this end.

22. After the next gate a ribbed concrete track descends to Great House, a government experimental farm between 1949 and 1982. Just before a gateway take the kissing gate on the right by an RW sign, and cut across the grass to the right heading for another gate and stile.

23. Follow the tarmac road past an old water trough fed by a spring, and where the road bends sharply left take a stile in the fence straight ahead. Cross the fields by a couple more stiles until a final one down on the left takes you back on to the tarmac road. (It seems hardly worth the effort but that is the public footpath.)

24. Just beyond the next farm, Trickling Water, the tarmac gives place to a stony surface and leads to Fall Bank, where traditional stone roofing slabs have been used in renovation work – and very fine it looks. Take a path to the right of the garage, pass through a gap in the wall and then through a gate. The RW now goes alongside a wall to a superfluous stile at the end. Drop down slightly to the ruins of Spring Bank, where water still flows from an old pipe.

Alden Brook crossing

Robert Pilkington once farmed here. According to a local story he came to be known as 'Rough Robin' because when he was asked what the weather was going to be like he always replied, 'A bit rough'. Ian Goldthorpe's Book 'Rossendale Rambles' describes the fascinating history of the 'Township of Pilkington' as the farmer termed his holding, and as most Helmshore-bred locals still call it. All along this section there are fine views eastward to Cowpe Lowe and Scout Moor.

25. Beyond the farm the original track passed below a line of gnarled hawthorn trees but a fair path takes the RW slightly above them to a stile in a wall. Beyond it the path leads down to Alden Brook, where a crossing can be tricky after a prolonged period of rain. It is an excellent place for a snack and a rest.

26. Once across the brook the path ascends gently, crossing a small stream. Is this Alden Brook, the longest tributary of the main

stream, or is it the wider one just crossed? Rainwater draining from the hill has made a river bed of much of the track for the next 100 yards, carving out deep ruts. There is a strong case here for some piping and shuttering to direct the water at intervals down the hillside. No one inhabits the upper valley now, but you pass the ruins of a barn on your left known as Goose Pits, and there was once a farm nearby, Middle Doe, which has left very few traces.

27. At the wall corner at the top of the track there is a Peak and Northern Footpath Society notice. If you have time and the inclination, you can bear left down by the wall to view the Ellen Strange Monument and cairn. They reputedly mark the site where Ellen Strange was murdered by her husband or lover around 1750. The stone was added in 1978. There is a poem by Laura Barnes about Ellen Strange but I don't have permission to quote it here.

Moor Road, once an important highway, with Ironstone Delph down on the left

28. If you prefer not to visit the monument then you should take the path up to the right over the brow of Beetle Hill. What a view on a clear day! The panorama is probably the most extensive on the RW. To the north, Tor, Cribden, Pendle Hill, Ingleborough, Pen-y-ghent; to the east, Cowpe Lowe and Black Hill. Foe Edge and Scout Moor bring promises of the time you will pass that way, battling against rain and wind or tempted to sit in the sun by Waugh's Well and gaze across to where you are now. The Pennines are in view, with Knowl Hill to the right, and so round to Rochdale and Bury. The huge wind turbines built on Scout Moor in 2008 detract from the view, in my opinion.

29. Keep straight on to a Peak and Northern sign and then descend towards a wall corner and an RW post. The path drops down into a hollow, and after emerging it takes you down towards a wood below. At a cobbled track by a field gate turn left past some old overgrown spoil heaps known as Ironstone Delph. Some authorities think this is the site of a former bloomery, a type of

Watersmeet, Buckden Wood

furnace once widely used for smelting iron from its oxides. A bloomery was the earliest form of smelter capable of smelting iron.

30. Cross the old highway known as Moor Road and use either the gate or ladder stile to take you along the track past the wood. Further down on the left is a good opportunity for a bath, but not a hot one, I think. And so down to the main road.

    The Official RW continues opposite, and I describe the route in paragraph 31; but it is so unattractive and messy that I advise a slight detour, described in paragraph 32. Take your pick.

31. *Either.* Cross the road and take the lane down to a junction where an RW sign points you to the right. Watch for a stile immediately in the fence on the right or you may become mired in a slurry pit near the site of Higher Buckden Barn by a gate and a stile, which is the legal right of way. So cross the first stile, onto National Trust property, and turn left, making a wide circle to avoid the mess by the gate. The RW then passes over a stile, and then down to yet another at the edge of Buckden Wood. The stone steps beyond drop down to a wooden footbridge. There is a handrail, as the stone surface can be slippery when wet. The path rises to join another one where you turn left. (Now see paragraph 33)

32. *Or.* Cross the road and turn right. Take a stile leading down into Buckden Wood and follow the path down to where the official RW joins from the left, as described in paragraph 31.

33, This is one of the loveliest parts of the RW, especially in spring, with delightful little waterfalls below. The land was given to the National Trust by Colonel AT Porritt (see more details below). The path descends to a watersmeet, crossing to the north side by a stone bridge. The RW continues along the left hand side of a clearing to a stile, where you leave National Trust Property. Ignore the bridge on your right, and continue down towards the sound of rushing water. Shortly, a lovely series of cascades is seen down on the right. Note the stone drainage channels in the path, now neglected, and, lower down, the huge blocks of stone in the ancient retaining wall on the left. Pass through a metal gate and continue behind Buckden Cottage and a converted barn residence. Note the drinking trough in the wall on the left.

Waterfalls, Buckden Wood

34. Turn right, then left, passing under the bridge of the dismantled track of the Helmshore and Haslindgen section of the former Manchester to Accrington railway, which is now a public footpath providing an attractive walk to Irwell Vale. Immediately afterwards you go under the East Lancashire Railway line. This is a preserved railway operating a daily service between Bury and Rawtenstall. You are now in the hamlet of Strongstry. Like Chatterton and Stubbins further along it has medieval origins. Most of the houses in present day Strongstry date from the 19th century and were built by the Porritts to house their mill workers.

35. Leave the village along a lane beneath trees with the river Irwell on your right. Cross the bridge towards the delightful village of Chatterton, with playing fields on the right. This is a peaceful place now, but all hell broke loose here in 1826. Following a spell of relative prosperity in the early 1820s, trade slumped towards the end of 1825 and this coincided with a major upsurge in the number of power looms being brought into operation. Thousands of hand loom weavers became unemployed and even those still managing to keep their looms working were existing well below the breadline. Ignoring the reading of the Riot Act, a mob broke into the Chatterton factory, which stood where the recreation ground is today, and started to destroy the power looms, while others stoned the soldiers sent to stop them. Eventually, the riflemen were ordered to open fire; four men died instantly and many more were wounded. As the soldiers gave chase to the fleeing rioters, two innocent bystanders – one a woman – were shot dead. The remains of Chatterton mill and its lodge were demolished towards the end of the 19th century and in 1923 its site was made into playing fields and given to the people of Ramsbottom as a 'Peace Memorial'.

36. The road passes the church, and continues through the village to the main Bolton Road in Stubbins. The RW continues along the lane opposite.

The name ' Stubbins' means 'land covered in tree stumps', or a place from which many trees have been cleared, and goes back to the Middle Ages, when local people began creating farms out of the heavily wooded countryside. The building of a calico print works towards the end of the 18th century marked the beginning of the change to an industrial village. Its present shape began in the 19th by the building of rows of terraced houses for print workers. The Porritt family built Stubbins Vale mill in 1851. Colonel AT Porritt gave much of the nearby countryside to the National Trust in memory of his son, Richard, who was killed in the Second World War. There is an excellent chip shop just over the bridge on the right, open lunchtimes.

2. Stubbins to Cowpe Lowe (Waterfoot)

approximately 6 miles (9.4km)
(plus ½ mile (1km) to the road in Waterfoot)

This section of the Rossendale Way starts where the A676 crosses the River Irwell at Stubbins, along a lane between the old Bank Bleaching Mill and the river. For information about Stubbins please see the end of the previous chapter.

Peel monument on Holcombe Hill

1. In a few yards the lane turns sharp left up the hill towards Sheep Hey, where it turns right on to Leaches Lane, which then bends left to cross the M66 Motorway. Turn left and follow the road and in about 300 yards (274m) take a narrow tarmac path up to the A56, Whalley Road.

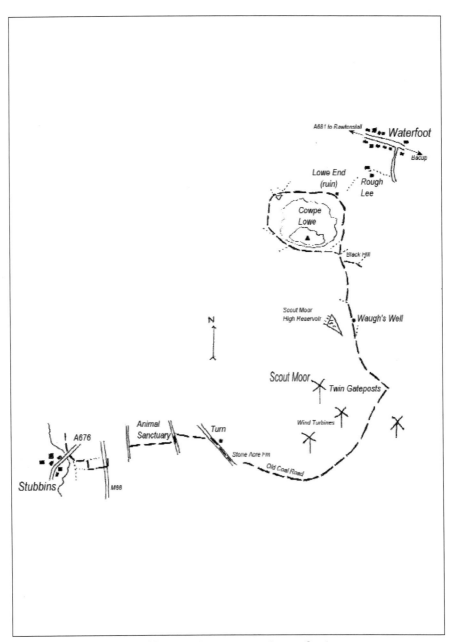

Stubbins to Cowpe Lowe (Waterfoot)

2. Cross the road and turn right, and then left after the last house. Ahead there is a fat man's agony stile, where you may need to remove your rucsack. A path alongside a wall then passes the Bleakholt Animal Santuary, where you may see donkeys, ponies, and interesting breeds of sheep and goats; you will certainly hear dogs! There are a number of saplings with labels attached commemorating pet owners' dogs or other animals that have died.

3. You emerge on to Bury Old Road. Turn left for a few yards, and then right up Bleakholt Road. This is quite narrow, and at weekends is often lined with parked cars whose owners are visiting the Animal Sanctuary.

4. At the top you reach Rochdale Road and turn right. The first house you pass used to be The Plane Tree Inn, providing snacks and meals: no longer. When you reach a spot opposite the drive to Stone Acre Farm, keep straight on to the bend in the road, ignoring the OS 1:25 000 map which does not show the alteration to the footpath. Cross the road at the bend and ascend wooden steps into a field. Go straight ahead to a stile in the hedge, cross it and turn right. The path here can be very boggy even after a dry spell. The building you see down on the right is known as Lime Leach, and housed weaving looms in the eighteenth century.

5.

Carry straight on up the green lane, once paved in places. The track is part of the old Coal Road. Coal from the collieries on Scout Moor used to be brought along this lane, but once the tramway from the collieries down to Turn village had been built the road fell out of use.

6.

The RW joins a lane coming up from Fecit Farm at a notice welcoming walkers on to Access Land. The track is in excellent condition, being well drained initially on the moorland side, with strategically sited culverts to carry the water away down into the valley. Unfortunately, as on many old trackways in the hills, it is now in no one's interest to keep the ditches clear, so higher up the lane rainwater often runs down, causing surface erosion. When the wall is reached, take a look over it.

Scout Moor from Turn village, before the coming of the turbines

The Cheesden valley down to the right opens out: the site long ago of a number of water mills, the ruins of which would provide interesting exploration. Chris Aspin is of the opinion that Cheesden Valley is 'perhaps the most concentrated memorial in Lancashire to the once all-powerful waterwheel'. Starting with a fulling mill in the 1780s, there were later 15 spinning and weaving mills along the six miles (9.5km) of Cheesden Brook to the outskirts of Bury, with a community of several hundred people. Great Lodge, the site of which you will pass later, ensured adequate supply for the mills. One of the mills had a 36ft (11m) wheel, and Cheesden Pasture Mill on the edge of the moor was the annual venue for Handel's Messiah, and even had a pulpit. The moor above the other side of the valley is Knowl Hill.

7. Shortly after the wall drops down to the brook, there are some rocks which provide excellent shelter with a superb view down

the valley. Unfortunately, high above you are the whirling sails of one of the many wind turbines erected in 2008, and for the next mile the hum and swish of these monstrosities mars the usual natural quiet of the area. As you near the summit of the road, notice a pretty waterfall down on the right if there has been rain recently. Then a huge stone gatepost is passed, beyond which the surface of the track becomes eroded and more of the giant wind turbines appear. Scout Moor is on your left and Higher Hill on the right as you pass the site of Great Lodge reservoir, constructed around 1840. The dam was removed in 1984. On sunny days in spring skylarks can be heard.

8. Cross the road made for the wind farm construction traffic. As you reach the summit of the pass, two huge stone gateposts, roughly hewn, stand before you. On dark days of low cloud these appear quite suddenly and starkly out of the mist, for all the world like two ancient megaliths. Should you pass between,

Old Coal Road, once used to bring coal from the Scout Moor collieries

perhaps risking transmigration into another world? The choice is yours, as it is possible to pass round them if you wish.

9. The path now descends, with a broken wall on the left, to a stream which falls over slippery slabs of stone into a deep clough on the left. It's no use looking for the footbridge indicated on the OS map: there is no sign of it now. The stream is one of many feeders of the Scout Moor High Reservoir below, that was built between 1903 and 1910. Further along, short, narrow board walks help you avoid very muddy ground.

10. When you reach a wide gap in a ruined wall, note the old trackway used to ascend to the right: the modern path goes straight ahead. This section of the walk lies along Foe, or Fo, Edge. Some say the name derives from 'Fall Edge'. There is another Foe Edge on the RW, on the north side of Haslingden Grane.

In the 19th century Cheesden Valley had numerous water mills

Gateposts at the summit of the Coal Road

11. Soon you come to Waugh's Well. A prolific Lancashire dialect writer, Edwin Waugh is said to have written his best work during his many visits to Foe Edge farm further down the track. The memorial was built over the spring which still gushes forth today, and was where the poet used to sit while he composed his verses. The stonework was built in 1866, 24 years before Waugh died, and is thus an unusual memorial. Waugh's Well has been well looked after, (excuse the pun), the original broken inscription being replaced and the whole rebuilt in 1966. A few plaques to other people with no connection to Waugh have been attached to it in recent years. This is an excellent place for a rest and lunch in good weather, with fine views over the moorland. Up on Scout Moor, a cross, in memory of a flying officer and Scout Group founder who was lost on a flying mission in 1955, is clearly seen against the sky. So, unfortunately, are the turbines. Looking north, Cowpe Lowe dominates the view.

12. Carry on along the track, which takes you to the scant remains of Foe Edge farm, 1371 feet (418m) above sea level, demolished in 1979. There is an information board.

13. The sites of two more buildings are passed. The first is Four Acre or Fourden, and then comes Slacks; in each case only a few stones remain. A concrete track joins from the reservoir.

14. Where the concrete track forks left, the RW carries straight on, initially over stone paving. The embankment of an old tramway can be seen up on the right, which used to carry stone from Cragg Quarry down to the valley. At a stone gatepost it is advisable to leave the track, because further along it has become inundated and a permanent pond has developed. Join the tramway embankment till you reach a tall signpost, where a track from Black Hill comes down from the right.

15. The finger post indicates the Pennine Bridleway in clear white lettering. The small yellow sign shows that the RW turns left towards a slab track by a wall. It then circumnavigates Cowpe Lowe. (At this point don't take any notice of the RW sign on the other side of the post: that way madness lies!) The 'official' route by the wall is often under water and rushes, so it is preferable to use the old tramway embankment again as it curves in the same direction avoiding the wet ground.

16. The tramway eventually joins the lower road, surfaced with thick stone slabs, in which grooves have been made over the years by the wheels of heavy carts: follow this. The tramway drops gently down into a cutting on the left. Continue along for some 300 yards (274m) to where the old sunken tramway once passed under Sand Beds Lane leading down the hill towards Edenfield. The tunnel was blocked many years ago.

17. Go ahead and cross a stile, and then bear slightly right along a green causeway to rejoin the tramway, which has curved round to the right, at a small waypost and a taller signpost. Turn right and continue through disused quarry workings, leaving the tramway just after some large slabs of stone on the right. Aim towards the raised bank of a small reservoir. Proceed along its

Waugh's Well

western edge, turn right at its corner and then drop down the bank, making for two huge wooden gateposts in a wall corner.

18. The RW now bears half right and crosses a pathless and very marshy patch of moorland and then a deep wide ditch, so a slight diversion from the official route is recommended here by following the farm track instead.

19. The track passes over a boggy patch, where an attempt to create a better surface with very large loose stones has not succeeded. The track then leads up over the breast of Cowpe Lowe. Where the track descends and becomes barely discernible, leave it on the right making for the corner of a low ruined wall and a rotting wooden post. New waymarkers are needed here. Continue with the ruined wall on your left. Soon the path runs

above the ruin of Lowe End and crosses an old water supply pipe.

20. Cross the stile down on the left. The RW continues along the base of Cowpe Lowe, but this section's description ends here.

To leave the RW here for Waterfoot, turn down the field to a narrow stone 'squeeze' in the bottom wall. Head straight downhill, taking as direction the church spire below. Soon a group of buildings comes into view: Rough Lee. Pass over a stile (not through the gate on the left) and go straight on between the buildings. The first one on the left is called The Manor House, dating from 1768. Take the lane to the right and then turn left at the junction by a picnic site. Turn left again at the next junction and follow the road down over the River Irwell, and you are in Waterfoot.

3. Cowpe Lowe (Waterfoot) to Healey

approximately 7 miles (11.25km)
(plus ½ mile (1km) from the road in Waterfoot to the RW)

The start of this section can be reached easily from Waterfoot. Just off the A681 on the road to Cowpe, immediately before the bridge over the River Irwell, there is a small area for parking. The Rochdale to Bacup railway line once passed over this site by the river. The passenger services on the Bacup line were discontinued in 1949. The final closure occurred in 1967 and there is little obvious evidence of the main line's former existence and residents of Waterfoot, for example, sometimes find it difficult to imagine what the area once looked like before the railway, its bridges and viaducts were demolished.

Waterfoot and Newchurch from above Rough Lea

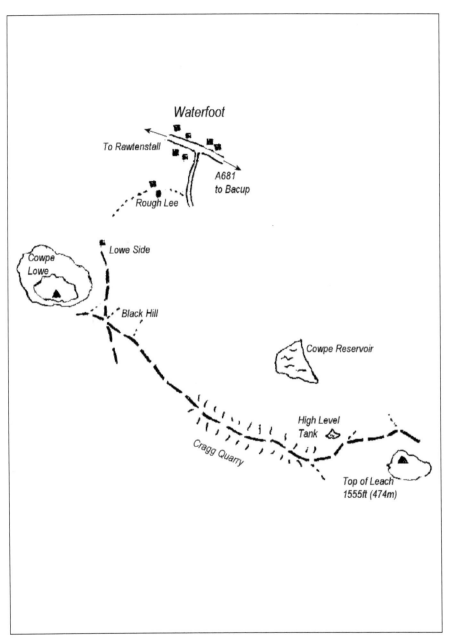

Cowpe Lowe (Waterfoot) to Top of Leach

To join the RW, cross the river, and follow the road as it ascends and bears left. Turn right at a sign to a picnic area, and then right again. Go past the picnic area up to a group of buildings known as Rough Lee. Turn left and pass between them. The second house on the right is known as The Manor House and dates from 1768. Beyond the buildings a stile takes you into a field, and it's a steep pull straight up. As the slope eases, go slightly right and make for a 'squeeze' stile between stone slabs in the wall up ahead. Continue up to the middle of the next field and fork left at some grassy mounds. There used to be a signpost here, as it is a junction of two paths, but it has disappeared. Along the top edge of the field below Cowpe Lowe lies the Rossendale Way.

1. Near the top of the field bear left to a gap in the wall. There is a stile here but it is hardly needed. There is a stream on the near side of the wall and very muddy ground.

2. Before you are the ruins of Lowe Side Farm. Take the stile in the fence and keep to the line of the old sunken track as it ascends steeply. Fine views of Cowpe Reservoir open up on the left, with Cowpe, or Kearns, Mill below the dam. Soon the track takes a sharp right turn to pass round the head of Lench Fold Clough. It is such a clear landmark it is surprising that it isn't named on the modern OS map.

3. Pass over the stile by a gate. A notice welcomes you to Access Land. Diagonally across the moorland to the left you will see a fingerpost and this is your destination. As you near it, notice the curved embankment of an old tramway on the right used to take stone from Cragg Quarry down to the valley.

4. The fingerpost has clear white lettering showing the Pennine Bridleway in both directions. The RW sign indicates left to the clear stony track up the side of Black Hill. (Don't be confused by the arrow on the other side, which indicates the RW in the opposite direction: it's for walkers coming from Scout Moor, who will then circumnavigate Cowpe Lowe.) Soon you arrive at a gate.

5. The surface of the road along a lot of this section consists of stone slabs, with grooves made by thousands of cartwheels when this

was an important highway — high in more than name as you are
now at about 1300 feet (410 metres) above sea level. The road
originally descended by the wall on the left, still a right of way.
We shall rejoin it later, after we have continued ahead through the
extensive workings of the disused Cragg Quarry.

6.   An old tramway route comes in from the right, a continuation of
     the one seen at the fingerpost. Further along in the quarry the
     tramway forks off to the right to the disused Ding Quarry, south
     of Top of Leach. Carry straight on between spoil heaps. The stone
     from here came to be known as Haslingden Flag, and some
     authorities say it was used to pave Trafalgar Square. There is the
     base of an information board in the quarry; either the board was
     never put in position or it has been destroyed by vandals.
     Scramble bikers visit this place at weekends in spite of notices
     about it being illegal to drive on a bridleway.

Cowpe Reservoir and High Level Tank from Cragg Quarry

The junction of the RW with Rooley Moor Road near Top of Leach

7. The trackway passes along the extreme edge of the quarry above a steep drop, but eventually descends to a lower level before it leaves the quarry by a ramp on the left. On the extreme left is a gate which leads on to a terrace above the upper Cowpe reservoir. There are more of the slabs of stone similar to those seen earlier, but here completely hidden under the turf. I was able to remove some of this to reveal that this was the continuation of the highway from Black Hill.

8. Turn right after leaving the quarry, eventually passing an old water tank on your right. The stone slabs are very deeply scored along this section of the road.

9. Continuing along, you arrive at the junction with Rooley Moor Road, also known as the Cotton Famine Road. The secondary name came about during the 1860s, when many impoverished cotton workers in Lancashire, instead of siding with the cotton-producing Confederate States in the US, expressed support with the Union's blockade – in particular for the abolition of slavery.

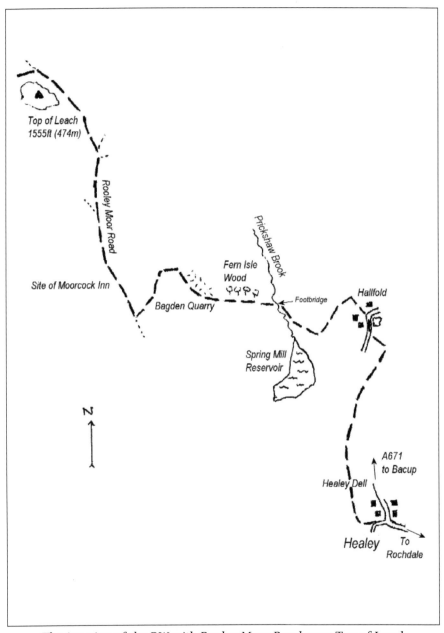

The junction of the RW with Rooley Moor Road near Top of Leach

This one-time much used highway has more of the large stone slabs along much of its length, as here, but further south these gave way to sets, laid as part of an early 'job opportunity scheme' provided by employers to help relieve the poverty of mill workers with no cotton to weave. Turning left will take you down to Stacksteads, but the RW turns right here, and soon arrives at the highest point of the whole Way: Top of Leach. Here on the right, easily missed, is a small stone monument, toppled on its side. It was erected to commeorate the opening of the Rossendale Way by the mayor on 28 April 1985. Representations to the authorities to have it restored seem to have fallen on deaf ears. Peak baggers might like to walk over the moor above to reach the true summit of Top of Leach, 1555ft (474m) above sea level, well worthwhile on a clear day for the extensive panorama. There is an unusually designed stone direction post (almost illegible), a small stone shelter and a trig column. I shan't elaborate on the disturbing presence of the wind turbines.

This Commemoration Stone to celebrate the opening of the Rossendale Way in 1985 has been so neglected that it now lies on its face

The true 'Top of Leach' is just a few yards off the Rossendale Way

10. After three quarters of a mile (1.2km), the old track to Ding Quarry is passed on the right. It is a tribute to the skill of the road makers that, for much of this length of the road, the surface is still almost as good as new. There are even kerb stones along its edges, although most of them are now covered with peat and moorland grass. In this area on the high moor there were a number of coal pits and collieries in the early nineteenth century. Most of the old tracks leading to them have been covered by the moorland grasses. After a quarter of a mile (0.4km) the site of Moorcock Inn, situated at about 1324 feet (404m) above sea level, is reached. A welcome refuge for travellers caught out in winter storms but, buffeted by the prevailing westerly gales and drenched with driving rain, this inn must surely have been an

unenviable place in which to live. It used to do a roaring trade, though, when many locals went 'on the rant', spending their hard earned money in just a few days. It was still named as an inn on the 1929 six inch OS map. All that remains today are two stone gateposts on the west side and a ruined field wall. Where did all the building stone go? I have read that the buildings, in ruins by 1968, were used for artillery target practice. Catching the eye to the west is the beautiful curved dome of Knowl Hill, 1375 feet (419 metres) high, above the Naden valley and its reservoirs.

11. Where the road dips before Windy Hillock with Top of Pike beyond, the RW leads off to the left. The sets are left behind but the track has a good wide surface. To the east there are views of Rushy Hill, Brown Wardle, Middle Hill and Hades Hill, over which the RW passes. Further east still the outline of the Pennines can be seen on a clear day, where there will almost certainly be walkers 'doing' the Pennine Way.

One view of the extensive Bagden Quarry, a pleasant place to explore

Prickshaw Brook from the RW above Fern Isle Wood

12. After about 600 yards (550m) look for a ladder stile in a dilapidated wall over to your right. There was a signpost by the track when I was last there but again, due to neglect, it has disappeared and there seems to be no intention of the authorities to replace it. When you reach a spot by some rushes directly opposite the stile a very faint path can be picked up leading towards it. Very marshy ground and a stream are encountered just before it is reached. Cross the stile.

13. The RW now goes through a gap in the stone slab fence on the right to recross the stream. These stone slab fences are a common feature of the Rossendale area, many of them being held together by the insertion of bolts with diamond-shaped plates.

14. There is no visible path initially, but by keeping to the edge of Bagden Quarry you will avoid most of the marshy ground. The

large quarry fell into disuse many years ago, but below you will see piles of roofing flags, huge blocks and kerbstones, as though they are still awaiting shipment to building sites.

15. As you round the end of the quarry cliff top, drop down to a track coming out of it. You can find shelter from any wind by turning left into the quarry, which is interesting to explore and a good place for a lunch stop. It is strangely peaceful.

16. To continue on the RW, outside the quarry follow a line of rushes down the steep slope towards Fern Isle Wood. A faint path can be picked up which crosses a broken wall and on to a kissing gate in the corner of a fence. Cross it, but take care, as there are a few spiked stumps of an old iron fence sticking up along the path beyond. It is possible that 'Fern Isle' should be 'Fern Aisle', referring to the long narrow shape of the wood.

17. Soon the path joins a clearer track which leads up to the ruins of two farms on the right, Robin Bank and Neck o' th' Bank, but the RW descends round the hillside to a footbridge over Prickshaw Brook, which flows into Spring Mill Reservoir.

18. Climb to the clear track above, known as Danes Lane. To the left, it continues to the bottom of Fern Isle Wood, crosses the brook, and so on to the ruins of Withens Farm. The RW, however, ascends right to a stile. Note the large stone in the wall on the right, where an inscription, almost totally illegible, 'AEH 1680', refers to Andrew Hoyle and Elizabeth (Rainford) Hoyle who were married in 1679.

19. Danes Lane, now between walls, takes you up to another gate and stile, where the RW turns left past farm buildings known as Houses o' th' Hill. Keep straight on as the lane descends, and just after a left hand bend look for a narrow footpath forking down to the right between private gardens and a wall. After a few yards go down steps, turn right, and descend the steep road into Hallfold Village.

20. Just before school buildings, look out for a large stone in the garden wall of a cottage on the left dated 1618 with the initials EI and H. It was taken from a nearby building, now demolished.

21. Cross the road at the junction with Wallbank Drive. The gravestones lining the edge of a grassy area on the left are all that remain of Hallfold Presbyterian Chapel and burial ground. The original building was constructed in 1710, replaced by a larger one in 1849. It was in this cemetery that the body of one of the banknote forgers mentioned in the next chapter was buried, but nothing remains of his grave today.

22. Just past a mill lodge turn left. The lodge was used to provide water power for Mill House Mill, a dyeing and finishing works which stood just below. The OS map of 1890 labels the mill as disused but it was not demolished until the 1960s. The lodge has been turned into a pleasant feature of the residential area. There is an information board describing it.

23. Take the right hand path through the wood over a short length of boardway and turn right at a crossing path. After the path leaves

Hallfold Reservoir stored water for Mill House Mill below

the wooded area, turn left and pass over a stone bridge which used to span a railway track. Then turn right to walk along the line of the old railway, which the RW now follows to Healey.

24. Continue on past where the Mary Townley Loop of the Pennine Bridleway goes off to the left and soon reach a gate. The lane coming down from the right had a tramway by which stone was brought to a rubbing mill, the remains of which can be seen on the other side of the gate. There is an information board telling you about it.

25. This area by the river Spodden is known as Healey Dell, and there is a Nature Reserve. Further on, notice some steps on the right leading up to a road. Across it, although not actually on the RW, the Broadley Wood Mill site is both an interesting and pleasant place to explore. There is an information board relating the history of the mill, and if you ascend the steps behind the site you will find the mill pond, now a quiet and delightful spot to sit and relax.

26. Back on the RW, proceed along the line of the railway track, and you arrive at the old Broadley station platform. There is an interesting notice here relating the history of the line. East of these sidings among the trees is the site of the former Broadley Mill, disused by 1890. Carry on under a road bridge until you come to the Healey Dell viaduct.

27. The Lancashire and Yorkshire Railway Company constructed a branch line from the south to Broadley station through Healey Dell beginning in 1865, and this necessitated the building of this huge viaduct. It is 103 feet (31.5 metres) high. Beyond the Broadley Station we have just passed, the line reached the former Dye Works mentioned above. The passenger services on the Bacup line were discontinued in 1949 after which only coal trains were operating. The final closure occurred in 1967.

28. At the other end of the viaduct, going straight on and then turning right will take you to the Nature Reserve Ranger's Office. Healey Dell is worthy of a visit at any time of the year. It has a wide range of flora and fauna, its own Fairy Chapel and a rich industrial past.

The Healey Dell Visitors' Centre houses exhibitions and organises walks. It is rich in wildlife, with a fascinating archaeological history. There are a number of websites dealing with this lovely area. Typing 'Healey Dell' into the Google search bar will reveal them.

29. For the RW, take the steps on the left down to a road and turn right. At the top of the hill you reach the junction of the B6377 with the A671 just south of Broadley.

    The RW continues over the road along a narrow lane called Ending Rake.

4. Healey to Sharneyford

approximately 7 miles (11.25km)

This section starts opposite the junction of the A671 with the B6377 at Healey, about 1¼ miles (3km) south of Whitworth. There is room for one or two vehicles on the north side of the B6377 opposite the toilets (avoiding the bus stop area).

The archway in Ending Rake, Healey

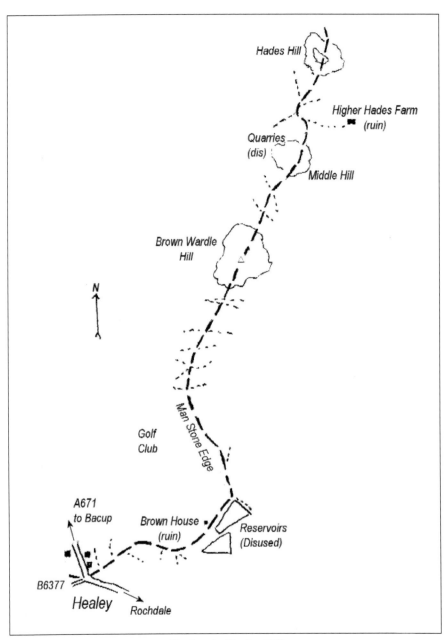

Healey to Hades Hill

1. Take the lane named Ending Rake. It leads under an arch, through a gate, and on to a cobbled track alongside a wall on the right. This is a lovely section of the RW. As the track proceeds it passes a site on the left where there was a shooting range in the 19th century used by the Rochdale Volunteers.

2. After passing some bungalows, cross a concrete drive and continue ahead along a stony track with another wall on the right. Soon you come to the ruins of Brown House below Rushy Hill. Robert Shore once lived here, a man fond of playing cards with his friends. There is a story that one night while they were gambling, they were scared out of their wits by a loud clattering in the chimney, and they thought the devil had arrived. They later found the noise to have been caused by righteous neighbours pouring turnips down the chimney! There were once two reservoirs below Brown House, but the smaller of them, Hamer Pasture Reservoir, is now just a dry hollow, and the larger, Brownhouse Wham Reservoir, although with a little water in it today, went out of use in the 1990s.

Brownhouse Wham Reservoir below Robert Shaw's ruined house

3. Continue along the track, which descends to a crossroads. Turn
    left, soon passing below Man Stone Edge, where it is said that Lord
    Byron, then Lord of the Manor of Rochdale, and his lover, Mary
    Chaworth, used to stand in 1803 for the views over to Blackstone
    Edge on the Pennines.

4. At the next junction bear right towards the steep slope of Brown
    Wardle. Cross a tarmac road and walk straight on, shortly
    bearing left through a cutting in an old tramway embankment.
    Turn right and head up the slope towards one of the many
    boundary stones you will come across on this section of the RW.
    Ahead of you is the steepest climb on the whole RW circuit. Over
    200 years ago the pioneering Taylor doctors set up their practice
    in nearby Whitworth. 'On a fine autumn evening early in October
    1764, a strong handsome young man with an oaken walking
    stick bearing a bundle of clothes over his shoulders, walked
    along the moor at the foot of Brown Wardle...he had walked that
    day from Halifax...' (from 'The Taylors of Lancashire,
    Bonesetters and Doctors, 1750-1890' by John L West). John
    Taylor was formerly a blacksmith and horse doctor. He lived at

Man Stone Edge

The signpost at the foot of Brown Wardle Hill. It may or may not be there: signposts along the RW are subject to sudden disappearance

Whitworth House, just below the Red Lion pub. The Whitworth doctors were local bone setters but also treated patients from London and overseas, including the then Archbishop of Canterbury. Climbing the steep slope of Brown Wardle was a favourite cure that the doctor often prescribed for those who lacked appetite and exercise.

5. RW walkers not lacking in stamina are ready to hare up the hillside, roughly following the line of boundary stones by one of a number of eroded 'paths'. Pause on the brow of this fine hill to take in the wide views. On the western side of Rushy Hill, almost due south, is Meadow Head Farm, and west of Hodge Hill (really a low spur of Brown Wardle) the ruins of Intack Farm. These were the former homes of two forgers, James Cudworth and Gilbert Holden, who printed bank notes. They were tried on 14 August 1809, found guilty, and hanged in November. Rushy Hill itself was once the scene of foot races, wrestling and also bull-baiting and cock-

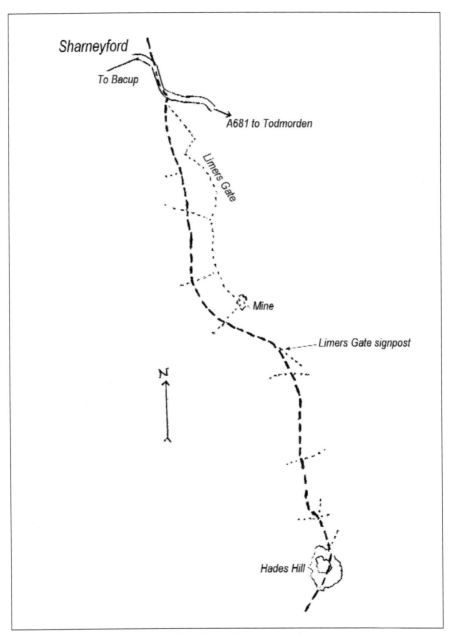

Hades Hill to Sharneyford

fighting. The events attracted up to 2,000 spectators and competitors, and beer tents were erected by local publicans. Puncing (kicking) contests were held, where contestants wore clogs, and the injuries were often very severe, and occasional fatal. Today the sport taken on the hill is slightly more peaceful: golf! Over on the far side of the valley can be seen the slopes of Rooley Moor along which the RW passes to its highest point of the route, Top of Leach. Beyond the moor Knowl Hill is the most prominent height on the skyline, apart from the two dozen huge wind turbines.

6.   Follow the wide track over to the cairn on the summit of Brown Wardle. You have a very good view of the route the RW takes over Middle Hill and on to Hades Hill.

7.   Before you descend the steep northern slope look across to plot where the path goes up Middle Hill, as it isn't clear from down in the bottom. It slants diagonally up to the right across the facing slope of Middle Hill to the corner of a broken wall fence, seen

Middle Hill seen from Brown Wardle

easily from this vantage point. You will probably encounter some wet ground in the saddle below.

8. Head up to the corner of the wall, from where a path leads over the eastern shoulder of the hill. Many old quarry workings can be seen in the valley below, mostly grassed over now, and Watergrove Reservoir is seen to the south-east. As you round the hillside, huge spoil heaps come into view. You follow the path down to the foot of them (more wet ground), with the ruins of Higher Hades Hill Farm down on your right. As in Haslingden Grane, remote farms like Higher Hades were the places to buy illicit whisky, or home-brewed ale known as 'burgy'. Now there is nothing left but a pile of stones.

9. Pick your way around the base of the spoil heaps. The path then becomes indistinct. Head straight uphill on the intermittent path between the spoil on the left and rushes on the right. At the top of the slope you will see a path going right, a couple of yards before you reach a quarry track. Turn right on the path until you see a boundary stone on the left, which you should make for.

10. Beyond the boundary stone, turn right along the distinct quarry track for a few yards and then turn left to ascend a faint path up Hades Hill. There used to be signposts here, but again, as in other parts of the RW, they have disappeared. Head on up the track past piles of stone heaped around an old quarry. The RW continues over the shoulder of the hill on a clear track; but a detour left should be made to the lumpy summit. Excavations here have revealed the remains of a Bronze Age barrow, dating from around 1300 BC, and archaeologists think there are others in the area waiting to be uncovered. There are good views in all directions, westward into the Rossendale Valley over Shawforth and Bacup, and particularly to the east where on a clear day Stoodley Pike can be seen, a major landmark on the Pennine Way.

11. Resume your journey on the track to a metal gate. Go through, turn left, and follow the fence to a stile where you enter a long, wedge-shaped field. Cross westwards to the path on the other side and continue by the excellently built wall, continuing direction

when the path enters a wide lane (no gate), ignoring all stiles and gates on the left.

12. At the small gate at the top end of the lane, the RW enters a field. In the distance, almost due west, Knowl Hill stands out prominently, and the ground before it is the continuation of the Rossendale Way as it heads northwards for Top of Leach.

13. Through the next gate follow a path to a tall signpost with a Limers Gate sign and turn left alongside the wall. (For more about Limers Gates see the next chapter.)

14. About three quarters of a mile (1.2km) further on, a fence leaves the wall at an oblique angle following the county boundary, marked by more of the boundary stones encountered earlier. The RW continues alongside the wall. Climb over the barrier (neither stile nor gate!) and continue along the Way, again ignoring stiles on the left. A few minor marshy patches must be traversed, but just when the Todmorden to Bacup road comes into view ahead and you're thinking the going isn't too bad, take care! The next 50 yards (45m) along Reaps Moss can be very bad. Adopt Wainwright's maxim and watch where you're putting your feet. The only way to keep them dry is to totter about, flattening the thick rushes and trusting that they bear your weight. Then suddenly you are on drier, firmer ground again as you begin to descend. Just off the path to the right is a metal cross and a stone with the initials BB.

15. Take a stile by a gate, and then another leading on to a well-used track which takes you down to the site of the former Clough Head Brick Works and the main Bacup to Todmorden road. Turn left up the hill. Shortly, the Limers Gate and the RW can be seen leaving the road just past a lay-by on the opposite side, where stone and rubble have been piled to keep vehicles out. Follow this for only a few yards to a junction where the old Flower Scar Road goes off to the right beyond a locked barrier.

The RW continues straight ahead.

5. Sharneyford to Weir

approximately 1¾ miles (3km)

This short section starts near where the A681 Bacup to Todmorden Road bends round to the right above Sharneyford, where a stony track heads up to a car park with a height barrier on the right. Further up, the track to left and right carries the Rossendale Way. The barrier ahead was locked to prevent fly-tipping on the moor along the Flower Scar Road. Much rubbish illegally tipped there was cleared by voluntary workers from Todmorden and Bacup. Something similar is needed along the lane, to the left, where the RW runs northwards. The messy piles of rubbish and illegal tipping along the lane greatly detract from the pleasure of walking this section of the RW, but there is no alternative route.

1. Walk along the lane to the left, ignoring the forking track at another barrier. This lane and extensions of it north and south, is one of the Limers Gates. 'Gate' is the northern English word for road or track. Many of the tracks across the bleak moor tops originally formed part of a network of paths for packhorse trains. The wet valley bottoms were difficult for travellers, and Galloway ponies used to pass along here loaded with sacks of lime from Clitheroe to be sold to those who farmed these acid upland pastures. Lime was — and still is — important for improving the poor Pennine soil. There are a number of Limers Gates shown on the South Pennines Ordnance Survey map.

2. At Heald Top, pass through the farmyard. Just past the farm buildings turn left through a gateway in the broken wall. Go straight ahead to a signpost and gate and turn right, then follow the broken wall and fence to a stile. Proceed ahead, keeping a wall on the left. A fine example of quoins can be seen in the ruin of a seventeenth century barn once named Heald. There are remains of sandstone quarries on the right, where the local workers produced stone flags and ashlar blocks. The weathering of ashlar

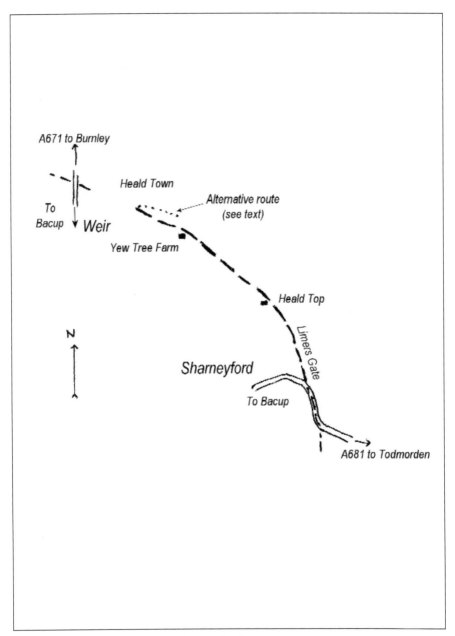

Sharneyford to Weir

enhances the natural beauty and emphasises the intricacies of the stone. The stone was used for heads, sills, mullions, quoins, corbels, balustrades and copings.

3. Soon after the next building on the left, you come to an eighteenth century barn once known as Old Tree. Note the old drinking trough on the right. Carry straight on through the next gateway, ignoring the track to the left.

4. Take the track which ascends slightly. Building and other alterations at Yew Tree Farm, the next building, involved a diversion of the farm track and in consequence the RW. The owner of the house has installed an electronic system which prevents his dog from approaching the public footpath, but I am unsure whether the dog had agreed to this, so I advise keeping to the public footpath above the fence! This leads through old quarry workings and then drops down parallel with the lane beyond the farm and joins it further along at the end of the next field. It's a slight diversion from the official RW.

Apart from this memorial, few traces are visible of the old chapel at Heald Town

5. Note on the left the lodges (reservoirs) of the former Irwell Spring Dye Works, started in 1833. The route now passes between buildings. The new residence here on the left is on the site of the former Black Butt Farm. The cluster of buildings just beyond is what remains of Heald Town. The 1841 census reveals that it was occupied by some 107 people — a thriving community, where most of the men worked in the quarries. The majority of the buildings date back to the late eighteenth century.

6. At a junction of paths, take the narrow lane ahead between walls. A large memorial stone on the right marks the site of Heald Wesleyan Meeting House and School. Pass through a metal kissing gate. The RW carries on over grass kept neatly trimmed by the owner of the next house.

7. As the lane turns left, a beautifully carved wooden sign points the RW walker down the lane. Unfortunately, this is not the official

Looking back to Heald Town and beyond from the Bacup Road near Weir

RW. It seems odd, but you need to walk up the private drive ahead as if you were visiting a bungalow. Watch for and descend signposted steps almost hidden down in the hedge on the left and pass through a gate, turning right alongside trees. Down on the left the infant River Irwell gushes under a fine old arched bridge.

8. Take the gate ahead and pass between low walls on an overgrown path onto another private drive, and after passing a house on your right you emerge on the lane that the signpost indicated earlier. Take the steps and a small gate into a steeply rising field, cross the stile ahead, and continue to the top of the second field. A stone step stile near a small decrepit brick building, situated on the site of the former Deerplay Colliery Depot which closed in 1968, takes you in a few yards out on to the A671 Bacup to Burnley road just north of Weir village.

The RW continues along the road to the right for a few yards and then over it to a small gate in the wall opposite.

6. Weir to Clough Bottom

approximately 2 miles (3.25km)

This section starts just north of Weir and a quarter of a mile (1.2km) south of the Deerplay Inn on the A671 Bacup to Burnley road at a wide grass verge on the west side. Parking is not viable on the roadway here, but opposite the Deerplay Inn there is room for a few vehicles at the junction of the main road with Bacup Old Road. The Rossendale Way can be joined where the Bacup Old Road crosses it just to the south.

1. Assuming you are starting on the A671, enter a field by a wooden gate at the public footpath sign. Go up some steps and cross the small field to another wooden gate. Proceed up the next field with a wall on the right. Pass to the right of Height End and then on to the lane beyond. At a crossing of tracks you have reached Bacup Old Road. Cross it (or, if you have come along the old road, turn right) and continue along Harrow Stiles Lane.

2. At Harrow Stiles Farm take a gate on the right side of the buildings and continue, first with a broken wall and fence on the left, down towards where the path crosses a ditch. The RW then continues to a ladder stile, and then to Clifton Farm ahead. The landowner here has provided RW signs, so follow these through a gate (with height restrictions!) on to a lane and turn right. The track leads to the ruins of Star, among nettles and piles of rubble.

3. Turn left at the ruin and locate an RW signpost a few yards away. In summer this might be difficult if the grass is very tall. Once found, look half left and make for another post on the other side of the next field. Turn left for a short way, and cross a stile in the fence and immediately take another stile by a gate. Turn right alongside the wall and continue to a stone step stile, with the first step missing, in a wall corner. Fine views can be had over to the ever-prominent Cowpe Lowe above Waterfoot, with Peel

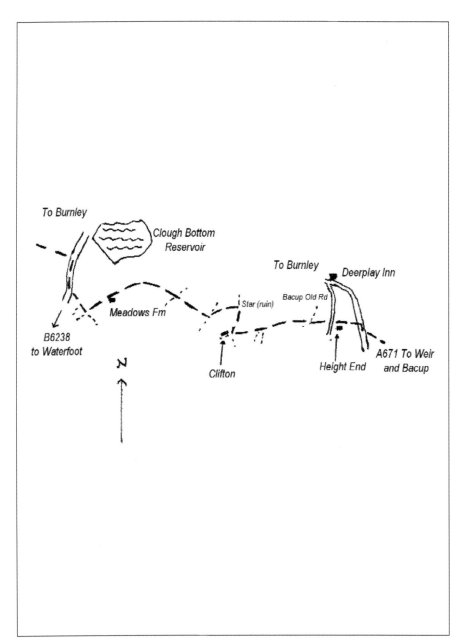

Weir to Clough Bottom

The unusual step stile above Clough Bottom reservoir

Monument just peeping above a hillside, and further right Bull Hill and then the masts on Winter Hill.

4. Soon you arrive at a tall well-constructed waterworks wall. Here there is an odd stile construction, one flight of steps over a low wall leading to another over a higher one. It's safer to go through the gateway, and you will then see that the higher wall was never continued, so you may pass round the end of it! Proceed with it on your left. Clough Bottom Reservoir, constructed by the Irwell Valley Water Board at the end of the nineteenth century, comes into view down to your right.

5. Recross the wall by the next stile where the wall makes a slight bend left. Continue direction in a rush-filled field for a short way to a wall gap, then turn half left on a faint path to a waypost. The OS map has the path crossing the broken wall and proceeding

along the left side of it, but changes on the ground have caused a path to develop to the right. So pass round the broken wall corner and head downhill to a stile which takes you to some wooden steps and down to a track at the entrance to the yard of Meadows Farm.

6. Opposite, a faint path leads to a few more steps, then the RW continues between a ditch and a fence. Pass through no fewer than four kissing gates, then through a wooden field gate at a wall corner, and turn right to yet another kissing gate.

7. Continue down a pleasant green track to a stile by a gate and then pass behind Lower Clough Bottom, over Whitewell Brook, and beyond this on to the B6238 Waterfoot to Burnley road.

    The RW continues to the right along a footway for about 300 yards (274m) and then crosses the road to a track almost opposite the Clough Bottom Waterworks buildings.

7. Clough Bottom to Love Clough

approximately 3 miles (5km)

Car parking space is hard to come by on the on the B6238 Waterfoot to Burnley road. Just north of Water village a lay-by on the west side provides a little space, and about quarter of a mile (0.4km) further north a space might be found at the reservoir entrance, but there are warning signs about blocking access. As an alternative starting point, but omitting some of the RW, see paragraph 4 in the text below.

1. The RW leaves the B6238 along the track almost opposite the Clough Bottom Reservoir buildings. Continue along it and, on reaching a crossing track, turn right through a gate up towards the site of Lower Cross Farm. This track is part of an old highway which came from Clitheroe through Burnley. At the next gate, notice a wall on the left: it marks the start of a short tunnel carrying a water channel under the track to Clough Bottom reservoir.

2. Cross the stile on to Access Land and ascend between high banks. The RW continues along a terrace with a water catchment channel down on the left which helps to feed the reservoir mentioned earlier. Continue uphill, the track clearly defined, ignoring a crossing track, to a signpost. Here the Pennine Bridleway goes off to the right.

3. The RW carries straight on in a deep cutting. As the track levels out, Compston's Cross comes into view ahead, an excellent place for a snack if you have come far along the RW today. The original cross, restored and moved to its present position by Alderman Samuel Compston in 1902, was situated nearby at 1154 ft (352m) above sea level. It was known as Higher Cross, and is now marked by a low upright stone. From the modern cross, look west to the left of a wall running roughly westwards and it can be seen against the sky. There was another at 1147 ft (350km), known –

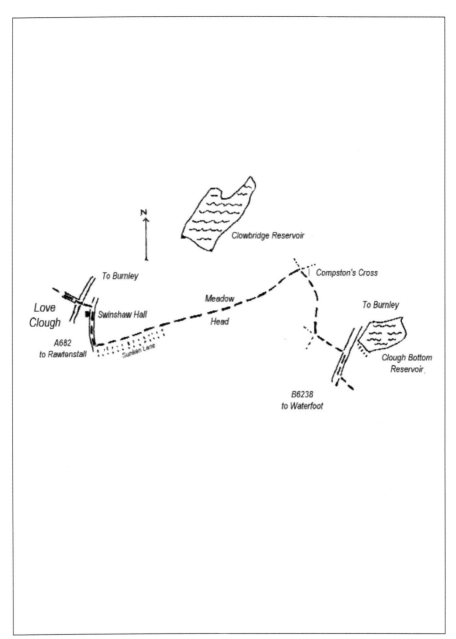

Clough Bottom to Love Clough

not surprisingly – as Lower Cross. The site of this one can be found by taking the higher of two tracks to the south and in about 50 yards (45m), after it bears right towards the line of pylons, a marker stone will be seen on the right in some rushes. The crosses were near the meeting place of four trackways, one an old route to Whalley Abbey. Crossroads used to be considered magical places, where strange, other-worldly events might happen, hence the positioning of crosses sanctifying the place. Pendle Hill to the north dominates the fine views from this point.

4. Access to the RW at Compston's Cross is easily made from the A671 Burnley to Bacup Road via a wide track over White Hill. There is ample space to park on a side road where there is a gate and direction arrows.

5. To continue the RW, go through the gate and turn left alongside a wall. The OS map shows the RW crossing a stile directly under the second line of pylons, but its continuation thence along the other side of the wall is difficult, so has fallen out of use. Instead, continue along the well-used path ahead, like thousands of other walkers over the years, parallel with the wall. This is a really fine, long stretch, easy-going as it's mostly on the level, with great views to the right over Clowbridge Reservoir to Nutshaw Hill and Pendle Hill, and as far north as Ingleborough on a clear day.

6. Eventually, the path passes through a gap in a ruined wall. Look left to see the stile where the official RW emerges according to the OS map. It now takes direction along a clearly defined path over Meadow Head, the highest point along this section of the RW at approximately 1197 ft (365m). It leads down to an access notice. Go through the gate ahead. Off to the left, below the well-constructed wall, are the ruins of Hillock Farm, and about a third of a mile (0.5km) further south the site of Swinshaw Colliery. A tunnel with a tramway linked it with Gambleside Colliery, which was adjacent to the southern corner of Clowbridge Reservoir to the north. At the end of the nineteenth century, there were seven active pits on both sides of the valley. The old hamlet of Gambleside dates back to 1242. Court rolls show that the colliery was working as long ago as 1612. Young boys called 'drawers', who were often as young as six years old, took the full tubs of

Compston's Cross

coal from the collier to the underground haulage system. Gambleside Colliery ceased production in 1936. Clowbridge Reservoir is now a popular location for outdoor activities such as water sports, fishing and orienteering. There are walking and riding trails throughout the area.

7. Continue along a pleasant green causeway with a wall on the left. After a gate and stile, where the old track descended straight ahead by the wall, long since out of use and overgrown with rushes, head slightly left, and cross another stile. The right of way goes alongside the wall on the left, but the practical route now crosses the old lane on stone flagstones through the rushes and continues high on the right. In the fields below on the left, there used to be the Green Fold Reservoir but this began to leak and was drained in the early 1980s. You have a good view of where the RW continues over Goodshaw Hill straight ahead.

8. As you descend, you reach an area where, curiously, trees have been planted over the course of the old lane. The stile is still there but it is not much use to walkers, as fighting one's way through a dense plantation is no fun. The officials who put the RW waymarkers here must have been having a laugh! Follow the much-used path by the fence to the right and drop down to a kissing gate, then turn right on Goodshaw Lane.

9. Carry on along this tarmac road and after about a quarter of a mile (0.4km) you will pass Swinshaw Hall. This was formerly a dowry house for Towneley Hall in Burnley and there is a chapel over the main entrance for the Towneley family. The Towneley family themselves have lived in the Burnely area since the mid-thirteenth century. The present structure dates from 1847 although the site goes back to the early sixteenth century. There is said to be a subterranean passage between the house and Towneley Hall. 'Swinshaw' means 'wood of the pigs'.

10. In a few yards, take the stile on the left, and keeping right under the trees descend the field to a small wooden gate. The path leads to a flight of steps beside a building which was once Love Clough National School, built in 1846 and now converted into a private residence. You have reached Love Clough (or Loveclough) on the

busy A682 Rawtenstall to Burnley road. The RW continues along Commercial Street opposite.

There are two explanations for the name Love Clough. Meaning 'Lufu's Gorge' and known as 'Luffeclogh' in the year 1473, the area is said to have been named after a man named Lufu, who was possibly a tribal chieftain or elder. Alternatively, Love Clough means a valley where water lies. The land around was once a Royal Hunting Forest, but was transformed into cattle farms known as vaccaries during the reign of Henry VII. Love Clough was valued at £5 in 1604. Evidence of Stone-age settlements can still be found around the hilltops together with coal and lead mining. In the more recent past, the inhabitants of the farms and hamlets in the area supplemented their income by various textile crafts, including hand weaving. Today, much new housing can be seen on land where a printing business used to stand, started in the

Clowbridge Reservoir seen from the RW on Meadow Head

nineteenth century. There used to be a trout farm, and a new enterprise seems to be redeveloping it. Data has been recorded at the weather station in Love Clough since 1989, with continuous recording since the year 2000.

8. Love Clough to Rising Bridge

approximately 3 miles (5km)

Love Clough is a small village about 3 miles (5km) north of the centre of Rawtenstall on the A682 Rawtenstall to Burnley road. For more details of the area see the end of the previous chapter. There is roadside parking at the top of Commercial Street, which is just off the west side of the main road.

1.   The RW leaves the main road along Commercial Street. Below the terraced houses the name changes to Pennylodge Lane. Bear right at the bottom, cross the bridge over Limy Water, and follow the

Looking back over Love Clough towards Meadow Head

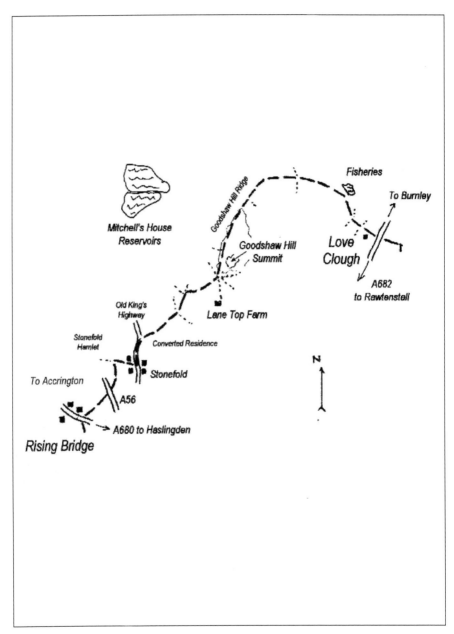

Love Clough to Rising Bridge

lane past new houses built on the site of the former print works. In a few yards the lane bends left behind them, and then the RW turns sharp right up a rising lane, soon coming abreast of fishing lodges on the right.

2. Take the stile on the left by a field gate and continue up the right hand side of the field. At the top pass through a kissing gate. Near here over to the right was the Goodshaw Hill Colliery, to which air-shafts that you will see later were connected. The colliery closed in 1932.

3. You have a choice of routes here. To follow the official RW, cross the stile on the left and ascend to a metal field gate. Beyond, locate a stile to the right of the renovated farm building and climb the hillside above it to a short waypost. Alternatively, you can use a concessionary footpath that the landowner has commendably created to avoid the farmhouse. This path runs from the kissing gate up the hill between the fence and a ruined wall; the disadvantage of this route is the long grass and rushes, which in wet weather will soak a walker from waist to foot. At the top of this alternative path, look for a short post on the moor above, where the RW is rejoined.

4. The post indicates three paths. If you have come up from the farm you turn left; from the concessionary path you go straight on. Shortly, the faint path levels out on the ridge of Goodshaw Hill and makes for a wall corner ahead. Cross a substantially built wall stile made from ornamental gateposts and turn left to follow a clear path. There are good views from along this ridge. Behind you is Hameldon Hill (with the masts), and to its left Great Hameldon. Further left again are Mitchell's House Reservoirs in the valley below, built in the middle of the nineteenth century to serve Accrington. The fenced off areas you see to the right are the filled airshafts which were part of Goodshaw Hill Colliery, mentioned earlier. Over to your left above Love Clough, you see Meadow Head, where the RW runs, and the line of the Pennines beyond. Skylarks may be heard on sunny days in spring.

5. Ignore the ladder stile on your left, and pass an old quarry on your right. Take the next stile on the left (the official RW stile ahead

leads into a pond!) and resume direction past part of the track now permanently under water. Pass a real pond on your left, just before the track divides below the 1236 ft (377m) summit of Goodshaw Hill. Take the lower right hand track down to a field gate and stile on your right. Cribden Hill, over 1300 ft (396m) high, is seen to the left of Lane Top Farm ahead. To the right of this, in the distance, is Peel Monument on Holcombe Hill, then Bull Hill, and, a little nearer, Musbury Tor, and Musbury Heights, with Hog Lowe Pike peeping over Thirteen Stone Hill.

6. Cross the stile and descend the field to a stile in the bottom left corner. Turn right on a track alongside a fence. As you progress you will note that the track was once surfaced but has become overgrown. Cross two well-designed stiles. At the bottom of the third field, turn left along another track to a cattle grid, which you cross and turn right along Goodshaw Lane. This leads you on to

Stonefold hamlet

the old King's Highway by a residence converted from a disused water board pumping station, and so on into the small village of Stonefold. There are some interesting buildings here. Take a look at the one on the right just past a lane and a barn. There is a noteworthy inscription over the door of the eighteenth century house exhorting people to 'Go in peace and sin no more'. Next door was the George and Dragon pub, which is now a private residence.

7. Assuming you have no sins which would prevent you moving on, turn down the lane by the barn. This takes you down to the hamlet of Lower Stonefold. Turn left through a gate and at an RW post turn right and cross the field to an old stone bridge over a tiny stream. Don't cross it, but follow the path downstream to another little bridge and cross there to a 'home-made' gate.

8. Turn left, pass above a rushy hollow, then descend to another small gate in a fence (not the field gate higher up!) and go on through the next small field and then through yet another small gate on the right. Turn left through a kissing gate, down through a second one, and turn right on the road which passes under the A56 Haslingden to Burnley road. At the bottom of Northfield Road take the steps ahead up to the A680 Haslingden to Accrington road in Rising Bridge. The RW continues along Worsley Street opposite.

Rising Bridge used to be associated, like most places in the area, with the cotton industry and quarrying, but now perhaps more with the famous Holland's Pies company, which was established in nearby Baxenden in 1907.

9. Rising Bridge to Clough Head, Haslingden Grane

approximately 3½ miles (5.5km)

This section of the RW starts in Rising Bridge about one and a half miles (0.8km) north of Haslingden on the A680 Accrington road at the junction with Worsley Street. There is room for parking in Worsley Street between the Spice Room car park and the local primary school.

1. The RW leaves the main road along Worsley Street at the side of the former Rising Bridge Inn, which is now The Spice Room, an Indian restaurant. The street has some terraced houses dating from 1840. After passing Stonefold Primary School, where Dr Rhodes Boyson learned his three Rs, later becoming a member of Margaret Thatcher's government, you cross over the old railway bridge which spanned the cutting of the dismantled Stubbins to Accrington railway. In the late 1970s the cutting was filled in when the Haslingden bypass was constructed. Immediately bear right and go up the road past bungalows. Just beyond the houses you might be able to find raspberries in August and, further along in the hedge on the left, sloes in autumn.

2. You reach Roundhill Road by the Farmers Glory. Turn right for a few yards and then cross the busy road into Moor Lane. A military establishment was located nearby in the Second World War, and some of the concrete left after it had been demolished was used to repair the lane side wall. There are some fine views northwards to Pendle Hill and the Bowland Fells. Moor Lane farm is passed, and the walled lane climbs to a kissing gate and cattle grid. The RW, now on an unsurfaced track, turns southwards alongside a wall on the left.

3. After about 150 yards (137m), the track crosses a boggy area on a causeway and then passes through a short cutting. As Copy Farm comes into view, the RW crosses a stream, which is passing through a culvert under the road, and proceeds between high

Rising Bridge to Clough Head, Haslingden Grane

walls. Copy Farm up on the right was used as an isolation hospital early last century. A recently paved section over a repaired culvert comes next, and after passing by a boulder perched on two others, the lane ends at a stile and gate.

4. Beyond, the RW descends on a wide green shelf on the shoulder of Thirteen Stone Hill. There are views of the old Hutch Bank quarry and, in the distance to the right, Peel Monument, a familiar landmark along the RW, and Musbury Tor. At the bottom of the field by a stile, the RW turns sharp right on an old sunken lane. A path above the lane on the right takes you up to Windy Harbour Farm, where there are sometimes several incessantly barking dogs. Still above the lane, pass by two RW posts and then rejoin the well-defined, and often extremely muddy, track beyond the farm buildings. You may need to struggle with the much knotted string which ties metal hurdles or gates together in order to pursue your right of way, as there was neither gate nor stile at the

Looking back along the Rossendale Way from Priestentax

time of writing.

5. Continue along to the next gate. The mud could be more than ankle deep at the remains of Picker Hill, in spite of the cobbles and flagstones still in situ. You may need to climb up by the wall and pass behind the ruins to avoid the mud. Originally known as Pickering's, this is just one of the many farms in this valley which were abandoned in the first quarter of the last century. The average farm size in the Grane valley was 37 acres, of which probably seven were moorland grazing. Half of the farms had fewer than 25 acres, and were too small to be viable on their own. Most of the farmers were able to supplement their income with spinning and weaving until power looms were installed in large mills. Until 1830, the handloom was still more important economically than the power loom, but the roles reversed and by 1850 there were some 177,000 cotton power looms in Lancashire alone.

6. Soon, just after a stile in a fence, the lane drops between high walls, and then turns sharp left, heading down to a wood below. The Forestry Commission created areas of woodland in the valley below the intake walls in the early 1960s to see how the high levels of industrial pollution affected tree growth.

7. The RW continues along the hillside above the line of the old track, now overgrown. Cross a stream which descends into a gulley to your left. Keep straight on at a group of trees which, on a hillside in these parts, usually means that a farm once stood there. In fact here is the site of Priestentax, a name that is derived from Priest Intakes. Intakes were the fields claimed from the moorland. Note the old water trough cut from solid stone. The old Troy quarry, just off the RW down on the left, now softened by vegetation, has become a popular picnic site.

8. Pass through a kissing gate to join the Old Causeway, which, to the right, leads up over Thirteen Stone Hill. Examination of depressions in the turf by archaeologists indicate that the summit is the site of a circle of thirteen standing stones. A survey made in 1972 showed that the circle was 96 feet (29m) in diameter.

9. Turn left down The Old Causeway, and then right at the corner of a new fence, where there is a way sign on the third post along. (The RW used to drop down the Causeway for about two hundred yards (180m) to a gateway and the ruins of Troy Farm. However, extensions to Heap Clough Quarry have changed all that. In 2007 the water which had filled the quarry for many years was drained, and stone extraction re-commenced. The quarry was greatly expanded, and in the process the remains of Troy Cottages down by the wood, a landmark on this section of the RW, were utterly destroyed. The farm ruins and the stone steps leading down to an old sheep dip were of interest to local historians. Now the quarry is abandoned and flooded again.)

10. So turn right at the fence and follow alongside it. Pass through a wall gap and cross a short metal bridge over a deep ditch.

Deep Clough

11. A few yards further on, you come across a rushy swamp, where the only concession to walkers is a few flagstones, half submerged under oozing mud in dry weather but completely covered after rain. Beware! These are stepping stones, and do not form a continuous hard surface. The gaps between could conceal the remains of previous incautious walkers, waiting to be dug up in the future as bog bodies and displayed in a museum!

12. After safely crossing to dry ground, look right to see the ruins of Far Priestentax, and to the left, over the other side of Grane, the spoil heaps of Musbury Heights Quarry below the restored chimney. The RW ascends to a broken wall, and turns left alongside the fence down to the edge of the extended quarry. The RW may eventually be diverted to a line below the quarries just above the road, where walkers will not have the same magnificent views over the hills.

The Rossendale Way at the site of Foe Edge Farm above Jamestone Quarry

13. The RW is now clear ahead between the quarry edge fence and a broken wall. The next ruin, with its single tree, is of the former Black Hill Farm. According to Ian Goldthorpe, during the Second World War a small mock airfield was created on the moor between the ruin and the higher ground to tempt enemy bombers away from the mill towns in the valley. It's difficult to imagine this when looking at the site.

14. The route now drops steeply into Deep Clough, crossing a stream by a footbridge, and climbs steeply up again to the ruins of Dilly Moor Farm. Jamestone Quarry dominates the foreground scene to the left, now filled with water.

15. You will find some paving flags on the path as you approach a small ruin on the left, heading between broken walls towards a group of tall trees and another farm site. This was Foe Edge, taking its name from the steep hillside, a name repeated at another point on the RW between Scout Moor and Cowpe Lowe, visible from here on a clear day.

16. Go through the kissing gate. The RW continues along the old trackway behind the wall.

To leave the RW here, turn left down the field to a stile, on the other side of which is a small conifer wood and an information board about the quarry and its history. Take the path through the small wood to another kissing gate, turn right keeping along a fence, till you reach a field gate, and then turn left along a track passing the site of the short-lived Grane Brickworks. Follow the track to the car park, where there is a very good café and clean toilets. There is also information about Haslingden Grane and special events in Rossendale. The busy B6232 (not A6177 as on the latest OS map) Blackburn to Haslingden road passes the car park.

General Information

Maps

The maps in this book are for minimum guidance only. Anyone walking over private land and on the hills, even on public rights of way, should have an up-to-date Ordnance Survey map, preferably the 1:25 000 scale (old 2 ½ inch). The ones that cover the Rossendale Way are the Explorer 287 West Pennine Moors, and OL21 South Pennines.

If you have access to the Internet it is fascinating to check out the early 1:10000 map on the Mario site. Go to http://mario.lancashire.gov.uk/viewer.htm?categ=historic, and choose the First Edition OS 1:10000 map. Keep zooming to the Rossendale area. (It takes a bit of practice!)

Books

Some of the books mentioned below are now out of print, but they may be found in public libraries in the district and in second hand bookshops in places even further afield.

The History of Haslingden Grane. A valley, its landscape and its people. Published on behalf of the West Pennine Moors Area Management Committee by Lancashire County Council, North West Water, Bolton and Bury Metropolitan Borough Councils, 1991.

Grane Revisited. Four Walks Around Haslingden Grane, by Arthur Baldwin, David Dawson, David Openshaw, John Simpson. Rossendale Heritage Network, 1991.

Musbury and Alden. Seven hundred years of life and landscape, by John Simpson. Helmshore Local History Society 2008.

Lancashire Pamphlets Vol 1 Rossendale, by Nick Dunnachie. Milllgate Publishing Ltd 1987.

Rossendale Rambles. Including the Rossendale Way and selected town and village trails, by Ian Goldthorpe. Rossendale Groundwork Trust Ltd. July 1985.

Further Rossendale Rambles. Being part of the Irwell Valley Adventure comprising a selection of walks from stations on the East Lancashire Railway, by Ian Goldthorpe. Rossendale Groundwork Trust Ltd, 1991.

The following books contain some information about walks in Rossendale.

Manchester Moorland Hikes, by Nick Burton. Sigma Leisure, 2000

West Pennine Walks, by Mike Cresswell. Sigma Leisure 1992

Walks On The West Pennine Moors, by Gladys Sellers. Cicerone Press 1978

Walking Northern Railways Vol. 2: West, by Charlie Emett. Cicerone Press 1989.

Public transport

Most of the starting and finishing points of the sections of the RW in this book can be accessed by local bus services. Both those listed below have web sites from which time tables can be downloaded as pdf documents.

Rossendale Transport Limited, (Easyride)
Rossendale Transport Limited, Knowsley Park Way, Haslingden, Rossendale, Lancashire BB4 4RS
Tel: 01706 390 520, Fax: 01706 390 530
Email: info@rossendalebus.co.uk
Web site: www.rossendalebus.co.uk/services.html
The only place that Easyride does not serve is Love Clough, for which see Burnley & Pendle Travel, below.

Burnley & Pendle Travel Ltd.
Queensgate Bus Depot, Colne Rd, Burnley BB10 1HH
Tel: 0845 60 40 110
Email: enquire@burnleyandpendle.co.uk
Web site: www.thewitchway.co.uk

Also from Sigma Leisure:

The Heritage Trail
Tom Schofield

The Heritage Trail is a 54 mile walk within the counties of Lancashire and Yorkshire, the route of which connects three preserved steam railways — the East Lancashire, the Keighley and Worth Valley and the Embsay to Bolton Abbey. The Trail is divided into 16 linked circular stages ranging between 4 and 9.5 miles.

£8.99

Coast to Coast on the Ravenber Way
A walk across northern England from coast to coast
Ron Scholes

The walk described in the book follows existing rights of way in the form of footpaths, bridleways and tracks, making this cross-country route a challenging long-distance journey. The walk commences at Ravenglass, it passes Lakeland's finest array of high peaks, climbs over the high Pennines, traverses the northern moors and ends at Berwick-upon-Tweed. Foreword by Betty Wainwright.

£9.99

Discovering Manchester
2nd Edition
Barry Worthington

This stylish walking guide doubles as a detailed account of the city's architecture, its history and tourism attractions. There are walks throughout Manchester including such major entertainment and cultural centres as the Bridgewater Hall, Urbis, the Museum of Science and Industry, the Lowry and many more. Explore the entire city – from the Corn Exchange to G-Mex, from the Cathedral to Affleck's Palace.

£10.99

Wirral Walks
100 miles of the best walks in the area
Anthony Annakin-Smith

A collection of 25 walks from around 2 to 10½ miles, covering a total of 100 miles through the best of the local landscape. The walks are arranged in order of length, with the finale being a shore-to-shore trail from Parkgate to Eastham.

The author's careful research highlights the interesting and unusual features seen along each route.

£8.99

All-Terrain Pushchair Walks
Lancashire
Kathryn Woods

The 10th in the highly successful 'All-Terrain Pushchair Walks' series. 30 Graded walks around the county of Lancashire, from level routes on high fells and wild open moorland, ancient woodlands and forestry plantations, delightful riverside rambles and bracing coastal paths. There are scarcely any obstacles on any of theses tried and tested pushchair-friendly routes with accurate gradings and at-a-glance symbols to help select suitable walks.
£8.99

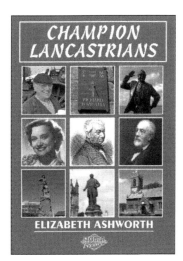

Champion Lancastrians
Elizabeth Ashworth

The 'Who's Who' of Lancastrians! This well-researched up-to-date, illustrated book features fifty notable Lancastrians throughout history including Emmaline Pankhurst, Gracie Fields, Eric Morecambe and Fred Dibnah and others rarely heard of who have made a lasting contribution to society in a variety of areas.
£7.95

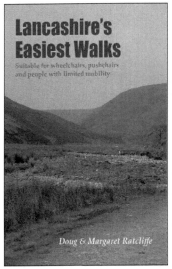

Lancashire's Easiest Walks
Suitable for wheelchairs, pushchairs and people with limited mobility
Doug & Margaret Ratcliffe

Lancashire and surrounding area has become far more accessible for wheelchairs and pushchairs in recent years. Although essentially a book for wheelchair users, these 36 specially selected short walks are all equally suitable for people with limited mobility and for very young children. Many of entries also have a 'points of interest' section describing features that can be seen from the paths and the photographs included illustrate the fact that a wheelchair or pushchair is no barrier Lancashire's wonderful scenery.

£8.99

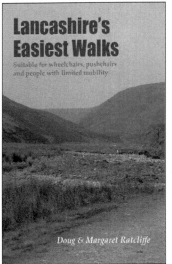

Exploring the North Peak & South Pennines
25 rollercoaster mountain bike rides
Michael Ely

This book will inspire you to pump up the tyres and oil the chain for some excitement, exercise and a feast of rollercoaster riding as you join Michael Ely on some great mountain biking in these Pennine hills. Over 500 miles of riding for the adventurous off-road cyclist that explore the tracks and steep lanes in the Pennine hills. There are twenty-five illustrated rides - with cafe stops half way round - to provide both a challenge and many hours of healthy exercise in classic mountain biking country.

£8.99

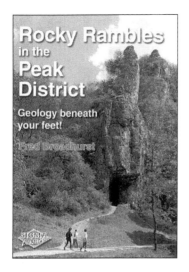

Rocky Rambles in The Peak District
Fred Broadhurst

"The Peak District has a dramatic story to tell and Fred Broadhurst is just the guide we need." – Aubrey Manning, presenter of the BBC TV series 'Earth Story'.

You don't have to be an expert or even an amateur geologist to enjoy these 'rocky rambles'! Where better than in and around the Peak District would you find geology right there beneath your feet - all you need to know is where to look.

The comprehensive glossary of terms, which covers the identification of Peak District Rocks, forms an invaluable supplement and provides 'at a glance' information for the reader.

£8.99

Peak District Walking On The Level
Norman Buckley

Some folk prefer easy walks, and sometimes there's just not time for an all-day yomp. In either case, this is definitely a book to keep on your bookshelf. Norman Buckley has had considerable success with "On The Level" books for the Lake District and the Yorkshire Dales.

The walks are ideal for family outings and the precise instructions ensure that there's little chance of losing your way. Well-produced maps encourage everybody to try out the walks - all of which are well scattered across the Peak District.

£8.99

Archaeology Walks in the Peak District
Ali Cooper

Put on your walking boots, enjoy the superb scenery of the Peak District and enjoy a roller-coaster ride through history with Ali Cooper. Routes ranging from 3 to 12 miles explore Peak District sites where there are visible features in the landscape. Brief descriptions of the major finds on the walks are included, plus a bibliography for those who want to delve deeper.

"... a new authoritative book ... for a spot of time travel while out walking" – Derby Evening Telegraph

£8.99

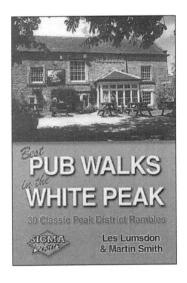

Best Pub Walks in the White Peak
30 Classic Peak District Rambles
Les Lumsden & Martin Smith

The 30 fabulous walks range from three to nine miles and ideal for family rambles. They start in such delightful Peak District villages as Ashford-in-the-Water, Alstonefield and Youlgreave, most of which are accessible by public transport — so that you can leave the car at home and savour the products on offer at the authors' favourite pubs.

Follow the recommendatios in this well-established — and completely updated — book for a superb variety of walks in splendid scenery and, after each walk, relax in a Peak District pub renowned for its welcome to walkers and for the quality of its Real Ale, often supplied by local independent brewers.

£7.95

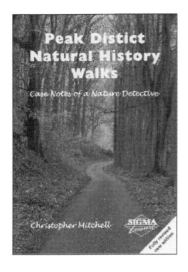

Peak District Walking Natural History Walks
Christopher Mitchell

An updated 2nd Edition with 18 varied walks for all lovers of the great outdoors — and armchair ramblers too! Learn how to be a nature detective, a 'case notes' approach shows you what clues to look for and how to solve them. Detailed maps include animal tracks and signs, landscape features and everything you need for the perfect natural history walk. There are mysteries and puzzles to solve to add more fun for family walks — solutions supplied! Includes follow on material with an extensive Bibliography and 'Taking it Further' sections.

£8.99

Best Tea Shop Walks in the Peak District
Norman and June Buckley

A wonderful collection of easy-going walks that are ideal for families and all those who appreciate fine scenery with a touch of decadence in the shape of an afternoon tea or morning coffee —or both! The 26 walks are spread widely across the Peak District, including Lyme Park, Castleton, Miller's Dale, and The Roaches and — of course — such famous dales as Lathkill and Dovedale. Each walk has a handy summary so that you can choose the walks that are ideally suited to the interests and abilities of your party. The tea shops are just as diverse, ranging from the splendour of Chatsworth House to more basic locations. Each one welcomes ramblers and there is always a good choice of tempting goodies.

£7.95

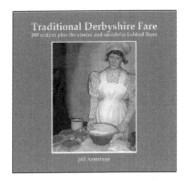

Traditional Derbyshire Fare
300 recipes plus the stories and anecdotes behind them
Jill Armitage

Some Derbyshire dishes are well known, like the Bakewell Pudding; many more, including some of the most delectable, are little known outside the places whose name they bear. The recipes are individual, easy, economical, with readily available ingredients, and have a strong regional accent. This is Derbyshire food at its best.

£12.95

Crime and Punishment in Derbyshire
over the centuties
Peter J Naylor

Crime fascinates us all, particularly murders, and the bloodier they are the better they are received. It would appear that the Peak District was a lawless place until more recent times. This book is a thorough mix of most of the types of crimes committed in Derbyshire over the centuries. Each chapter is dedicated to a different type of crime and the punishments handed out. Whilst this book gives much of its space over to murder, other crimes are also included.

£8.99

All-Terrain Pushchair Walks
Cheshire
Norman Buckley

30 graded walks, from level routes around pretty Cheshire villages to more adventurous hikes across the hillsides. Detailed directions and a map are provided for each route, together with some stunning photographs.

£7.95

Best Tea Shop Walks in Cheshire
Clive Price

"... A winning blend of scenic strolls and tasty tea shops." – Cheshire Life.

First published in August 1995 and sub-sequently updated with major revisions due to some tea shop closures and consequent re-routing of walks.

£8.99

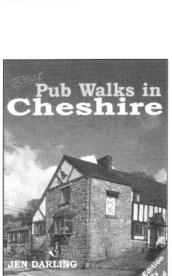

Best Pub Walks in Cheshire
2nd Edition
Jen Darling

This is the second edition of a guidebook to the walks and pubs of Cheshire.

"I was delighted to be asked to put a few words on paper ... this book brings together a series of suggestions for your enjoyment." – John Ellis, Cheshire Tourism

£8.99

The World of a Wainwright Bagger
Chris Stanbury

Chris Stanbury highlights the physical, mental and spiritual challenges the average walker will experience doing the 214 Wainwright fells, providing inspiration for those new to The Wainwrights, or to those who have done some of the fells but lost motivation along the way.

The walks are described from the standpoint of an average walker and are an excellent complement to the Wainwright Guides.

£8.99

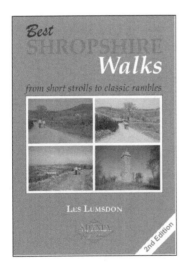

Best Shropshire Walks 2nd Edition
From short strolls to classic rambles
Les Lumsdon

A new revised edition of this much loved guide contains 36 walks, including 12 completely new routes, located in all parts of the county. Several walks feature fine hill walking on the Welsh borders and others start from delightful villages and hamlets in the north and east of the county.

£8.99

Beatrix Potter's Derwentwater
Joyce Irene Whalley and Wynne Bartlett

A fascinating look at the beautiful Derwentwater area as Beatrix Potter depicted in her sketches and books. Includes paintings and sketches by Beatrix Potter and photographs both old and new make this an invaluable book for visitors to the Lake District, and all those who know and love Peter Rabbit and his friends.

Detailed routes are included for three walks starting from Keswick so readers can explore the wonderful scenery found in the stories of Benjamin Bunny, Squirrel Nutkin and Mrs Tiggie-winkle.

£9.99

The Charlie Chaplin Walk
Stephen P Smith

Explore the London streets of Charlie Chaplin's childhood in a chronological tour that can be taken on foot or from the comfort of an armchair. This book concentrates on the story of Chaplin's formative years and takes a fresh look at the influence they had upon his films. For fans of Chaplin, those interested in film history and anybody with an interest of the social history of London's poor of the late Victorian and early Edwardian era.

£9.99

All of our books are all available through booksellers. For a free catalogue, please contact:

SIGMA LEISURE, STOBART HOUSE, PONTYCLERC, PENYBANC ROAD AMMANFORD, CARMARTHENSHIRE SA18 3HP
Tel: 01269 593100   Fax: 01269 596116

info@sigmapress.co.uk   www.sigmapress.co.uk